Needleweaving

...EASY AS EMBROIDERY

by Esther Warner Dendel

COUNTRYSIDE PRESS
a division of Farm Journal, Inc.
Philadelphia

Cover design: Al J. Reagan
Book design: Ann Churchman
Cover picture: weaving, Judy Whelan; photo, Frank Curcio
Back cover: doll, Beverly Nemetz; pillow, Helen Trescott;
     ornament, Patricia Holtz; Leo, Jo Dendel; mobile, Bici Linklater;
     bag, Lois Renwick; photos, Jo Dendel and Al Reagan
Black/white photos: Lee Payne and Jo Dendel except numbers
     3, 25, 29, 77 Al Reagan; 93 I. Serisawa;
     104, 114 Jean Stange; 115 Ed Walter
Color photos: Jo Dendel except numbers 9, 15 Al Reagan;
     10 Ed Walter; 13 I. Serisawa
Drawings: Jean Stange, Associate Professor of Decorative Arts,
     Arizona State University

Contents

A new way to weave

Perhaps we should say that this book tells you how to weave with a new kind of *loom*, because a piece of cardboard actually becomes your "loom". With a curved needle and almost any kind of yarn—plus Nature's offerings such as twigs, feathers, even seaweed—you can start this new craft.

Needleweaving is one of the most flexible and inexpensive of creative crafts. You can do the simplest weaving, or you can develop your artistic abilities as far as they will take you. You might even call this a freewheeling art form because it is so versatile and personal. It is an adaptation of the ancient craft of weaving that is fast becoming a popular medium of self-expression and pleasure.

Needleweaving is satisfying because you can share your creations in many forms. You can weave decorative accessories for your home, for your wardrobe, make gifts for friends, toys for children, Christmas tree ornaments . . . you can even weave greeting cards for very special people.

In this book you will find so much more than the techniques, although they are all here, step by step. (The artist-craftsman-author, Esther Dendel, is a teacher as well; she and her husband Jo, who shares her enthusiasms, instruct students of all ages in needleweaving and other craft media.) Because of the kind of persons they are, you will find their philosophy of earth's "friendship offerings" woven throughout the book. Mrs. Dendel says: "The home of a craft lies deep in the soul. . . ."

Even if you never put a strand of weft through warp, this book is bound to make you more aware of "art in everyday experience". In fact, Mrs. Dendel authored a book by that title.

Her own awareness had its beginnings on an Iowa farm. Later she was influenced by West Virginia mountain folk and African tribal craftsmen. She lived and worked with both of these peoples who had weaving as one of their basic crafts.

We believe this a unique book that can enrich your life and bring you a new adventure.

RACHEL MARTENS
Crafts/Home Furnishings Editor
Farm Journal

1. "Nature" tapestry by Virginia Weeks shows an appreciation
for things of the earth—cattails, seeds, lichen, tree bark, twigs,
driftwood and palm spathes are all woven into this wall hanging.

1
Why Weave?

Weavers will tell you that it is fun to weave. It is. But the delight of needleweaving goes deeper. Perhaps pleasure more nearly describes the feeling that goes with the work because pleasure and creativity are closely related. "With pleasure, life is a creative adventure; without pleasure it is a struggle for survival," Dr. Alexander Lowen observes in his book on *Pleasure*.

A large part of the pleasure of weaving comes from the fact that a weaver can make up his own rules as he goes along. The weaving thread follows the whim of the weaver as it meanders freely over the surface. You are not really creating if the rules have already been made by another. This is why stamped patterns (like games already made up) are less exciting.

Another great thing about needleweaving is that you can turn dreary time into play time— those hours spent under the hair dryer, waiting in a doctor's office or sitting outside the music room while your youngster has a piano lesson.

You probably glance at the clock and tap a nervous, impatient toe as your mind ticks off all those things still to be accomplished before the day is done. Waiting time is dreary and seems a waste. But not if you have some fulfilling handwork beside you. And there is a great difference here between fulfilling and time-filling.

Needleweaving can be carried about, transported to camp, beach, beauty shop or committee meeting. Chances are you won't notice how dull a meeting is when you're busy with your needle, and everyone around you will wish she were weaving, too! I once carried my needleweaving into a hotel lobby to wait for a friend and in five minutes I was teaching an impromptu class of people lured by the bright yarns.

A few years ago, I slipped on seaweed while photographing tide pools on the Big Sur coast of northern California. The nicest thing my husband brought me in the hospital was a cardboard loom and some yarn. When I remember

2. *Needleweaving is a hobby for all ages. Mike Hudson, age 12, designer and weaver of the lion pillow, shows his brother David, age 10, the wall hanging he is weaving on a cardboard loom.*

the year I was confined to a wheelchair following that accident, I recall my pleasure in all the needleweaving I did, not the misfortune of a broken leg. A year that might have seemed lost was in fact a year of personal growth and rewarding accomplishments with needle and yarn. I could not, of course, have used a conventional loom. The cardboard was light and fitted across the arms of my wheelchair and I worked in comfort.

There is a rhythm to the over and under, the in and out of needleweaving. When a weaver finds his natural speed, the rhythm that is right

for his own body, muscular tensions relax. Breathing, heartbeat, finger motion, a general physical feeling of well-being, all produce pleasure. Some would call this "therapy" (and it is) but I think "pleasure" is the nicer word.

Other people tell me needleweaving helps keep arthritic fingers nimble and in working condition. The yarns are soft and pliable and weaving is indeed a gentle art. It is satisfying for people in rest homes and convalescent homes; patients are sometimes able to sell their work. One woman who does not have any real need for money told me she had sold a needleweaving. Someone was willing to pay money for something she had made and she felt that she was not useless. How happy that made her feel!

To choose and use color is an outgoing action which confirms your self as a unique individual. You will, as you select the colors for your needleweaving, react to each color separately as you hold it in your hand; and to the group of colors acting upon each other when they are assembled. By letting your emotional response have full play, you will have provided an opportunity for personal growth.

Needleweaving is also a way to personalize and individualize your home in these days of look-alike houses on tracts. You may say, "*I* made that" or "I *made* that." Whichever your emphasis, you are making a statement about pleasure you have experienced in the doing—and will continue to have in the looking.

A needlewoven hanging is less likely to appear machine-made than a weaving done on a conventional loom. The cardboard or hardboard (untempered masonite) loom gives great flexibility to the woven product. So it is easier to do something spontaneous and imaginative in needleweaving than in regular weaving.

Another advantage of needleweaving over the conventional loom is the ease of storage. There is no room in the average home for a large loom.

And, finally, everyone can afford this type of "loom" for needleweaving—cardboard costs little or nothing and the hardboard for a 3x4' loom with leftover scraps for smaller looms costs a mere $1.25.

3. "Leather and Feathers" by Annabelle Bergstrom is a decorative neckpiece done in pheasant colors. It uses the plain weave only, but has 12 different weights, textures and tones of yarns—plus the bits of leather thongs and pheasant feathers.

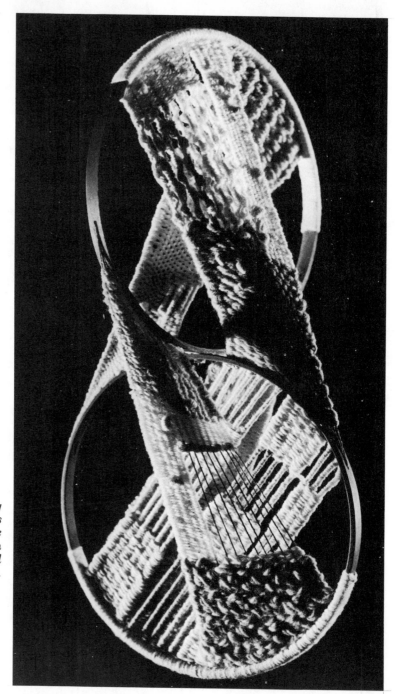

4. "Sculpture in the Round" by Phil Freeman uses two wooden hoops at an angle to each other. He attached warp top and bottom to yarn wrapped around the hoops; drilled holes for warp on inside curve.

Encourage the men in your family to try needleweaving if they seem intrigued; it is a creative adventure for the whole family together (Plate 2). Fortunately, men are feeling more secure about trying some of the home arts. A former football player of national fame shows off his needlepoint (a close relative of needleweaving) on TV talk shows, and it seems unlikely that anyone is going to call him a sissy. In many cultures men do all the weaving and there is no reason why men in our culture should forego this pleasure.

Young people who want to express individuality in their personal appearance can—with a needle, a bit of cardboard, some jute, fishing line or leather thong, a few feathers, driftwood or sea shells—improvise body coverings and collars that are minor works of art. Annabelle Bergstrom's "Leather and Feathers" (Plate 3) and Virginia Weeks' "Nature" wall hanging (Plate 1) are examples.

Like most of the weavers whose work appears in this book, Annabelle and Virginia are members of our Craft Fellowship. At informal meetings all year, we work toward our annual Craftsmen's Fair which now attracts customers by the thousands. We exhibit our own works, and also invite other craftsmen in the area to participate.

Happily for craftsmen, an increasing number of art associations throughout the country hold Crafts Fairs. Little Galleries are springing up like mushrooms and are looking for the unique crafts products.

There are other encouraging signs. Architects and interior designers visit our fair to choose one-of-a-kind hangings for their clients. Doctors and dentists come looking for something distinctive for their offices. Women who have not yet tried needleweaving themselves, buy hangings to decorate their homes. As each customer admires and touches a needlewoven wall-hanging, we can sense his pleasure in the luminous colors of yarn, the exciting textures of knots and loops, his satisfaction in bringing a well-done craft into his life and into his home.

Some of our weavings are choice, jewel-like little panels no larger than twelve inches. Others are twelve feet long—truly important decorations for lobbies and two-story halls. Many weavers of today are moving their work out from the walls, creating forms which can be viewed from both sides and in the round (Plate 4). Regardless of the size or purpose of the weavings, I feel that their greatest value lies in what the weaving has done for the weaver. This is the real answer to the question, "Why weave?"

5. Stuffed pillow dolls in all sizes and colors hang as mobiles— woven by Beverly Nemetz.

2

What to Weave

A belt, a collar, a necklace, a yoke,
A purse, a pillow, a carrying poke;

A greeting for someone special you like,
A blanket in squares for a little tyke;

A mobile to turn in the fitful breeze,
Unusual ornaments for Christmas trees;

A patch, a pocket, a band for a hat,
A room divider, a tie or a mat;

A circle to mark the sliding glass door,
And squares sewed into a rug for the floor;

Something unusual to hang on the wall . . .
You never reach the end or the all.

I often find myself humming as I weave. The rhythm and repetition of "under and over and on to the end" is a healing and pleasureful activity. As you see, it even prompts jingle-making.

And when your project is finished, you can proudly say, "I wove that." *What* one weaves is not as important as that one *does* weave, but this knowledge becomes a certainty only after you have mastered the technique of weaving.

Some people deny themselves the pleasure because they fear they do not have the patience to weave. Instead of soothing their shattered nerves, they are afraid weaving would fray them further.

Fortunately, there are big yarns and coarse fibers that work up quickly and with good effect. They are perfect for people who want things to move fast, or for children whose little

6. A belt in purples and pinks by Judy Whelan.

7. A collar in oranges and browns
with copper beads by Judy Whelan.

hands are not yet educated for fine work. Large yarns are no less beautiful for being rough and sturdy, and they certainly help the beginning weaver through the "getting involved" stage. Pleasure in your first small success in weaving deepens as you find you've actually "grown a little patience" too.

I do not believe that anyone is born with patience. I think patience is something each of us has to teach himself. We do well to compel ourselves, if need be, to do certain things which in the beginning, before we have mastered them, require a measure of patience. This pays great dividends as you grow older and find your physical energy in somewhat shorter supply. When life presents problems, the fortunate person is he who "can weave trouble away."

Once you have mastered a craft, you wonder why you thought in the beginning that it required patience. As soon as you find the rhythm of work and adjust it to your own body rhythms of heartbeat and breath, time flies. What seems like half an hour, providing you are conscious at all of time passing, will turn out to be three hours at least. Hunger and fatigue do not intrude. There is only the joy of the work. That is what is meant by being involved. The fragmentations of life have become reconciled into a calming kind of unity.

What one weaves may be almost anything that calls for a decorative fabric. It may be as small as a pocket or as large as a room divider. However, I see no point in weaving what can be woven more quickly and efficiently by a ma-

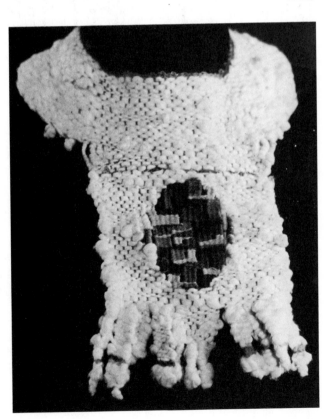

8. A yoke in coarse white yarns with a medallion of silky bright colors by Annabelle Bergstrom.

9. A pillow in green, blue and purple stripes by Helen Trescott.

10. A carrying poke with bead-trimmed fringe by Shelley Spring.

16

11. A 4-hoop mobile to turn in the breeze by Bici Linklater.

12. A Christmas tree ornament woven in a pair of embroidery hoops by Pat Holtz.

17

*13. Pockets of burnt orange and green, with
neck and sleeve braids to match, by Doris Fox.*

14. A tiny bright circle to mark a sliding glass door by Beulah Rollyson.

15. A folding screen to hide the kitty-litter box, by Eunice Ewing. Millard, the Dendel rabbit, models.

chine. If one is going to weave, why not weave original articles that do not come by the yard in fabric stores?

Most yardage, regardless of the weave, has the vertical threads at right angles to the horizontal. In needleweaving, one has the opportunity to interlace the threads in any direction. There is no need or reason to accept a boring machine limitation. By allowing the needle to roam at your whim in any direction, you become as free as a weaverbird, whose astonishing nests we would do well to study.

Gwen Frostic has stated this beautifully in her book, *A Walk with Me*. "Each bird has its own secret of nest building . . . but no bird has more than a bill to weave with . . . a foot to shape with . . . and its own body with which to mold the clay . . . and so with grasses, roots, twigs, bark, strings and mud they build their homes in which to raise their young . . . and line them with thistle, down, furs, mosses and feathers for comfort."

In our jingle, we list some of the things pictured in this book to tempt you. These projects are small in size, but big in imagination. Just as soon as you learn the basic weaves and knots (when you make your Tapestry Sampler—see Chapter 4), you will be ready to improvise and adapt designs for "unusuals" of your own.

16. *Handbag by Lois Renwick achieves textural interest by combining different yarns in a palette of many greens with sparks of bright red and yellow. Bag is lined with red silk.*

17. *Handmade greeting card by Tanya Baker. The mini-tapestry (3x8") attached to the card is handsome enough to frame.*

18. *You never reach the end or the all . . . Taurus woven over a shoe box—with one green eye, one blue—by Celia Wagner.*

19. This metal hoop loom remains a permanent
frame for the weaving—warp is threaded through yarn
covering the ring. Frances Schroeder, weaver.

3
Yarns, Looms and Needles

Needleweaving is not to be confused with stitchery or embroidery which are applied to a fabric that already has been woven. Weaving starts with a set of threads called warp, which are stretched, in our method, across cardboard or masonite. (Many kinds of looms have been developed over the centuries from a simple frame to complicated mechanisms—we are starting in the simplest possible way.) Weft is the thread that crosses and is woven into the warp. Because the more complicated looms may have a limiting effect on handwoven textiles, many present-day weavers have turned to the simple methods in order to gain freedom and flexibility in manipulating the yarns.

YARNS

First thing to do is collect a "library" of yarn in which to browse as you select the colors and textures you wish to use together. This need not be expensive. If you have friends who knit, probably they have baskets full of leftover odds and ends. Some yarn shops display sale prices on leftover single balls of yarn. You can unravel old sweaters and recycle them into your weaving. You can cut worn garments into strips, or you may be able to pick up scraps of fabric often available for nothing from upholstery shops to cut in strips; you may even want to unravel choice pieces for reweaving.

One outstanding weaver tells us he never be-gins a tapestry without collecting at least three textures of each of the colors he plans to use. If he has a texture he likes in white or in a light yarn, he will dye it to fit his color scheme, aiming not at a perfect color match but at something related to his scheme. If storage is a problem (and where isn't it?), fill a big salad bowl or a large basket with balls of yarn and use it as a color spot. An arrangement of yarn colors lifts the spirit and brightens the room.

For warp yarn, choose some kind that does not have much stretch. Carpet warp is a good cotton warp. Linen is excellent and in a four-cord twist is stronger than cotton carpet warp. Goat hair with a fuzzy texture gives an overall "bloom" to the finished work. My own preference is for dark warp. It gives a richness of color which one seldom achieves with white or light warp. You can see this in the illustration (Plate 21) where we have warped a cardboard half with light and half with a dark warp, using the same weft in both. In some cases you will want to use the same yarn for both warp and weft. But check yarn for both stretch and strength before you decide to use it for warp.

YOUR "LOOM"

Once you have yarns assembled, you need little else to begin. A cardboard or a piece of masonite slightly larger than the weaving will

23

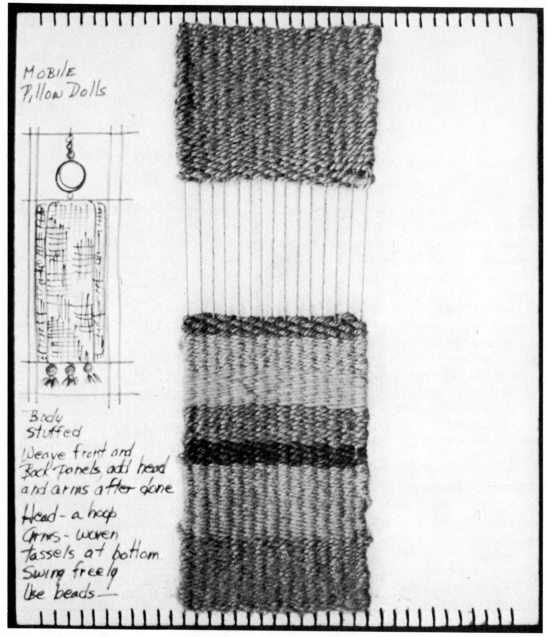

MOBile
Pillow Dolls

Body
Stuffed

Weave front and
Back Panels, add head
and arms after done

Head - a hoop
Arms - woven
Tassels at bottom.
Swing freely
Use beads——

20. To make a cardboard loom, cut slits ¼ inch deep and ⅛ inch apart
in both top and bottom. There is enough margin space to note weaving
instructions for Beverly Nemetz's mobile dolls shown in Plate 5.

be your loom. For a small weaving, stiff cardboard is adequate. A larger cardboard loom should be reinforced on the back with a second piece of cardboard cut slightly smaller than the first one—this will keep it from becoming floppy as you work on it. Cut slits in the edge of the cardboard with scissors or an X-acto knife to a depth of about ¼ inch. Good spacing for the cuts is usually ¼ inch apart. For a rectangular weaving, you need make cuts only in the ends of the cardboard (Plate 20). For oval or circular forms, you need cuts all around.

For large projects, untempered masonite makes a more satisfactory loom than cardboard. It may be cut or notched with a handsaw or power saw. You'll find it helpful to paint the surface white. This makes it easier to see what you are doing as you weave.

Perhaps the simplest loom of all is to cut slits in both ends of a plastic meat tray—this makes an excellent loom for a child (Plate 22). The small oblongs he weaves on it can be sewed together to make a blanket for a doll.

When you finish a weaving you usually dispose of the loom. But sometimes you will want to work on a hoop which becomes the permanent frame for your design. It might be a metal hoop, a little heavier than coat hanger wire. Use the buttonhole stitch to cover the metal with yarn and run warp threads through this stitchery (Plate 19). Or use a wood embroidery hoop, notch or drill it to hold warp threads (Plate 4).

21. Detail showing the effect of light versus dark warp threads when the same weft yarns cross both.

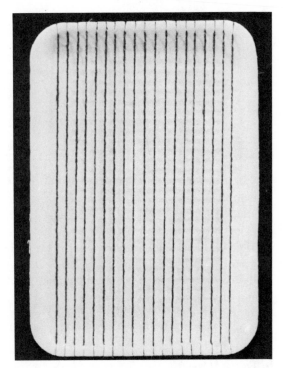

22. A plastic meat tray is easy to notch for warping, makes an inexpensive practice loom for children.

23. Ink the design onto the white background of the cardboard loom before warping it.

NEEDLE AND OTHER EQUIPMENT

A bent needle with a large eye is your first choice for needleweaving. If you cannot find a needle with a big eye which is also curved, you can curve it yourself with a pair of pliers. The needle will bend more easily if you heat it with a torch. Long bodkins are often handy, especially for plain weaves. You can make one: Drill a hole in one end of a long thin piece of brass; point the other end and bend it into a curve. You may find some Argyle sock bobbins useful, too, for carrying yarn.

You will need a tool for pushing the woven thread into place—technically called a beater. A dog comb is good for this, or you may use any large toothed comb. Sometimes your fingers or the weaving needle will be all you need to compact the yarns—especially for irregular or loose weaving. It is desirable to reduce equipment to the bare essentials, so that you as a weaver may turn your entire attention to experiencing the character of the materials themselves.

Obviously, you will need a pair of scissors. And if you are following a definite design, a felt tip pen will be handy for blacking in the design on your loom (Plate 23).

WHERE TO BUY SUPPLIES

Carpet warp and many of the other supplies you need are available through mail order catalogs or local yarn shops. If you have any difficulty, write to Denwar Craft Studios, 236 E. 16th St., Costa Mesa, California 92627.

26

4

Learning to Weave by
Making a Tapestry Sampler

There are three good reasons for making a tapestry sampler. First, by completing it, you will learn all the necessary knots and weaves. Second, you will see and feel what the different textures look like—the effects you can get; this makes your sampler a valuable reference for future work. And third, chances are you'll own a new wall hanging! Most samplers are handsome examples of needleweaving art you will be proud to display in your home (Plate 24).

HOW TO WARP A LOOM
FOR A SAMPLER

Cut a loom at least 12 by 18 inches from heavy cardboard. Cut slits on each end ¼ inch deep and ¼ inch apart.

Warp the loom with strong, non-stretchable thread (carpet warp or linen cord) using simple parallel warping, this way: Knot the end of the cord at the back of the loom, in the first slit near one corner. This knot simply holds the cord, keeps it from pulling out of the slit. Bring the warp across the face of the loom to the first slit in the opposite end, leading it to the back of the loom, then to the front again through the next slit. Continue leading the warp back and forth across the face of the loom, keeping warp in parallel rows and of even tension (Plate 25). Fasten warp in last slit with another knot at the back. (Note: The only warp thread that shows on the back of the cardboard loom will be the small stitch-like threads between the slits.)

If your yarn library holds rug yarn, this is a good inexpensive material to use for weft in a sampler, because it is large enough so you can see what you are doing.

24. Completed sampler of knots and weaves by Esther Dendel will become a decorative wall hanging when it is removed from the loom.

WINDING YARN

Wool is an elastic material and it should not be wrapped in tight balls—that takes the stretch out of it. Instead, wind yarn over two fingers as well as over the ball, to keep the winding loose. After a few turns, pull out the two fingers, place them elsewhere on the ball and again wrap over them. When I see a ball of yarn wound too tightly, I have an irresistible urge to rewind it, to liberate it!

THE WEAVER'S KNOT
AND CHAIN STITCH

Cut the weaving yarn about two yards long to start; you will get a favorite length as you work. If it is too short, you waste too much time re-threading your needle. If too long, the weaving yarn gets worn as you drag it through the warp. Use longer lengths of tightly spun yarn, but shorter lengths of loose, easily frayed yarn.

Anchor the weft (weaving thread) to the warp with a weaver's knot (Drawing 26, Plate 27). (Note: The photo also shows another way to warp a loom, leading two strands of warp through each slit—this would permit additional texture variations.)

25. Cardboard loom has ¼″ slits cut across top and bottom and is in the process of being warped.

27. Secure the weft to the warp with a weaver's knot.

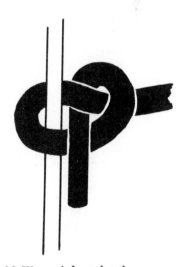

26. Weaver's knot detail.

29

28. *Start to weave near the center of the loom—allow your needle to roam freely.*

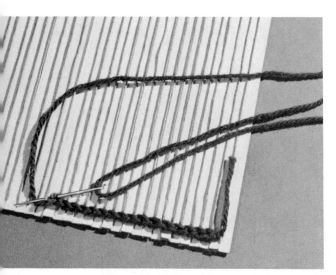

29. *Before you begin a weaving, put in a row or two of chain stitch at both top and bottom of loom— to space warps evenly and hold them in place.*

30. *Chain stitch detail.*

Place the knot for your first stitches at one corner of the loom and do a few rows of chain stitch (Plate 29, Drawing 30). The useful chain stitch helps space the warps evenly and holds them in place—do a few rows at the other end of the sampler, too. You will also use the chain stitch in the body of weavings to outline shapes. You can chain over more than one warp.

Caution: It is important, in doing any of the stitches, not to pull the weft too tight. Keep your eye on the warps, especially at the selvages; if they're pulling out of line as you weave, loosen up!

After you have done the "securing" rows at both ends of the loom, move to the central area (Plate 28). I suggest this because I find my students get more spontaneous effects this way, as I do. You have a sense of freedom, allowing the needle to roam freely among the warps in the empty center area, making curves and loops. This is a great plus of needleweaving and it is a mistake not to take advantage of it.

THE PLAIN WEAVE

Try your first curve in plain weave (some call this the darning stitch). Take your needle over and under about a dozen warp threads; then turn around and come back under the warps you first went over, and over those you first went under (Drawing 31). Both rows should follow a simple arc. Continue adding rows to the arc, enlarging it by including an extra warp thread each time you turn. When you have done about 10 rows (or run out of thread), turn your loom around and weave a matching arc in mirror-image relationship to the first (Plate 32).

You now have an oval-shaped opening between the two arcs. This is a good place to change color. Fill the opening with more plain weave, over and under, around and around, until all the warps are covered (Plate 33).

THE EGYPTIAN KNOT

When the weft loops around the warp, the result is a knot-type of weave. To make the Egyptian knot, study Drawing 35 and Plates 34 and 36. See how the needle dips each time under two warps—the warp being wrapped and the next one to be wrapped. Practice the Egyptian knot by putting in three rows of it from edge to edge of the sampler, and following the curve of the central medallion (Plate 37).

The tricky part is turning around, reversing direction. When you get to the turn-around, look again at Plate 34. It shows how you wrap the outside warp twice; then dip under and around the next warp; then continue as before.

At first, it may be a little difficult to get the tension right when weaving Egyptian knots. It helps to hold one finger on the warp thread that is being encircled, pressing it in place as your other hand draws up the weft thread. When the Egyptian knot is well done, every wrap looks like a beautiful little bead of yarn. When several rows follow one another, they produce a rib in the direction of the warp.

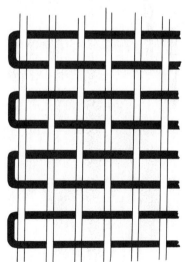

31. *The plain weave, easy as darning, is the basic stitch for needleweaving.*

32. Start sampler with plain weave in several rows of a graceful curve—turn loom around and repeat motif.

33. Fill in the center of almond-shaped medallion by going around and around with plain weave.

35. Egyptian knot detail.

34. Egyptian knot close-up showing how to turn around.

36. Weaving Egyptian knot next to the medallion.

37. Weave three rows of the Egyptian knot across the sampler, following the curve of the medallion.

1. Mandalas by
Frances Schroeder
Jean Robinson
Helen Dickey
Helen Trescott
Louanne Matsler

2. "The King"
by Esther Dendel
18x45"

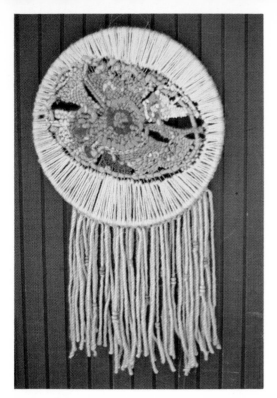

3. *Mandala*
by Jean Robinson
20" diameter

4. *"Pink Rock"*
by Louella Ballerino
12x20"

5. *"Sun Fish"*
by Lisa Bannies
12x26"

7. *Mandala*
by Louella Ballerino
14" diameter

6. *"Jubilee" and*
detail of turkey-bone fringe
by Tess Goldsmith
11x30"

9. Tablemat
by Esther Dendel
13x19"

10. "Rising Sun"
and detail of slit weave
by Roméo Reyna
4½x8'

8. Mandala
by Virginia Weeks
15" diameter

11. Mandala Screen
by Judy Whelan
frame by Jo Dendel
each square 22"

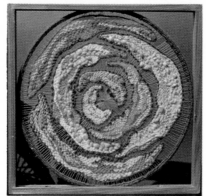

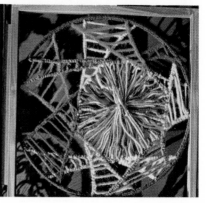

12. "Off and Away"
by Helen Hennessey
22x36"

13. Hoop Tapestry
by Tess Goldsmith
4x6'

14. Woven necklace
by Annabelle Bergstrom

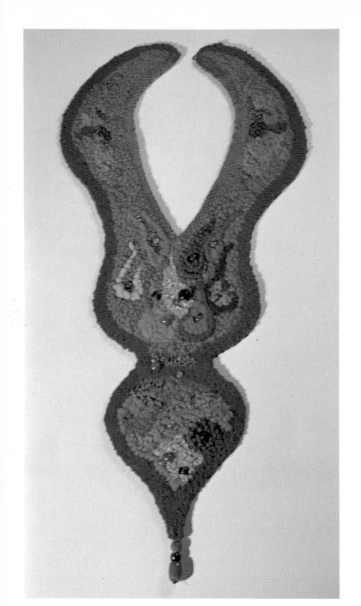

15. *Purple neckpiece
by Helen Hennessey*

*17. Dress and
mandala trim detail
by Rosita Montgomery*

*16. Red-red belt
by Judy Whelan
40" long*

THE TAPESTRY SLIT

In ordinary weaving, the weft yarn crosses the entire expanse of warp. But if you bring a weft only part way across the face of the warp and then turn back, you are beginning the tapestry slit. If you weave up to the slit from the other side and again turn around, you are bringing the weaving forward on either side of the slit. *It is this slit which defines tapestry.* In olden days, this was the device used to change from one color to another, and much effort went into sewing up the slits when the tapestry came off the loom.

In contemporary tapestry, the slits are added for decorative effect, usually without a color change. We make them on purpose and leave them open.

Slits in tapestry must be planned. If they happen just once in a while, or singly, they will look more like moth holes than decorative texture. I have seen tapestries where the slits were so well placed that I found myself thinking of them as notes of music.

For this illustrative sampler, I planned seven slits above the medallion in my sampler. They are placed to repeat and echo the curve of the medallion. I used a ruler to space them, and marked the placement of each one with a line drawn on the cardboard loom. You should do the same.

When you weave these tapestry slits, use the plain weave (Drawing 38, Plate 39). Decorative weaves would detract from the texture you achieve with the slits. After the slits are woven and you are ready to cross the entire area again, you may see trouble. That's because the over-and-under sequence of the plain weave may vary from one area to another. I solved this problem by making a few rows of the Egyptian knot. Use it freely any time you run into difficulty in the sequence of the plain weave.

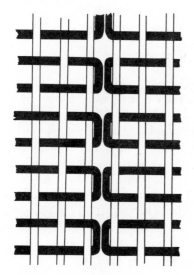

38. *Tapestry slit detail.*

39. *Tapestry slit close-up shows weaving both sides of the slit at the same time—with two needles.*

33

THE LOCKED SLIT AND THE DOVETAILED JOIN

You have filled much of the area above the medallion; now turn the loom around and work in the area below. Try weaving some simple shapes; I chose the shape of the capital letter "I", making three of them in the medallion color, using the plain weave (Plate 40). I also felt a design need to repeat the slits I used above the medallion, as you can see in Plate 24.

You can lock your shapes to the background with a single, interlocking tapestry slit (Drawing 41, Plate 42). Bend your two forefingers around each other to visualize this interlock. You may weave the shapes, and then weave up their sides with the background color, weaving each lock as you come to it. Or you may use two needles and bring the two colors forward at the same level. Instead of interlocking weft yarns, you could wrap each one around the same warp.

A variation on the locked slit is the dovetailed join (Plate 43) in which two or more rows of

40. Weave the I-shaped designs with plain weave.

weft are woven alternately around a common warp. The two colors meeting make a decorative serrated pattern.

SOUMAK LOOPING

If you have followed my sampler suggestions, you will have just a little space between the "I" shapes and the end of the loom, to fill with a couple of rows of Soumak looping. This is an Oriental stitch or knot, best described as being like the outline or stem stitch in embroidery, except you work it over warps instead of into woven fabric. You may go forward over two warps and back under one, or perhaps forward over four and back under two. You should alternate each row of Soumak loops with a row of plain weave; in this way, you will have all the loops going in the same direction (Drawing 44, Plate 45). Also the plain weave gives Soumak tapestry more durability and strength; this is especially necessary if you use Soumak for rugs.

Soumak can be made even more decorative. If you want a larger loop, work over a pencil which you pull out later. Or thread your needle with two different color yarns and use them as one—pink and red together, or blue and green.

THE GHIORDES KNOT

Another wrapped warp that will give you a lot of texture is the Ghiordes knot. Study Drawing 47, and Plate 46 to see how it is made; then practice a row of these knots above the slits in the top part of your sampler. You may cut the loops or leave them continuous; obviously, the fuzzy cut ends will provide more texture than loops. The Ghiordes knot is often used in rugs and is said to be named for an Anatolian village famous for rugmaking.

THE ALMOND MOTIF

While there are a few tapestry techniques yet to learn, you have mastered the basic ones, and

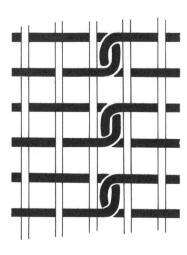

*41. Lock-stitch detail—
use it where two colors meet
to avoid an open slit.*

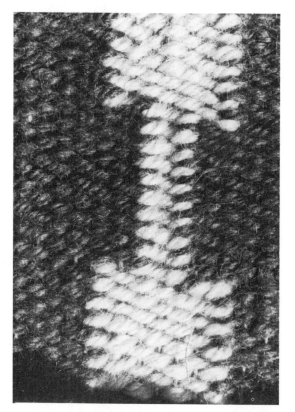

*42. Lock-stitch close-up—used where
background meets I-shaped design.*

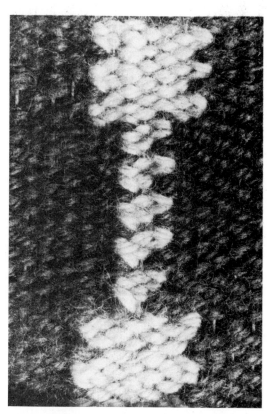

*43. Dovetailed join, where two or more rows
of background weft are woven alternately on
same warp as the outside edge of "I" motif.*

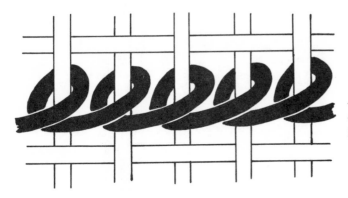

*44. Soumak looping detail—
alternate with a row of
plain weave for stability.*

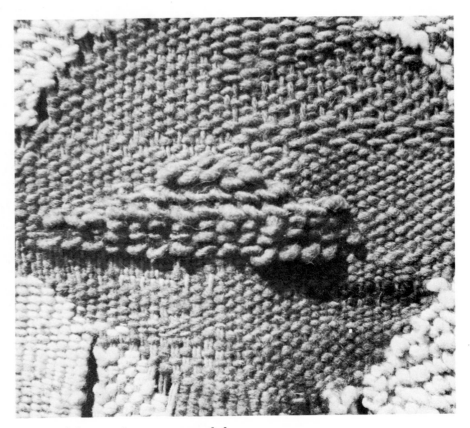

*45. Soumak looping close-up, surrounded
by areas of plain weave.*

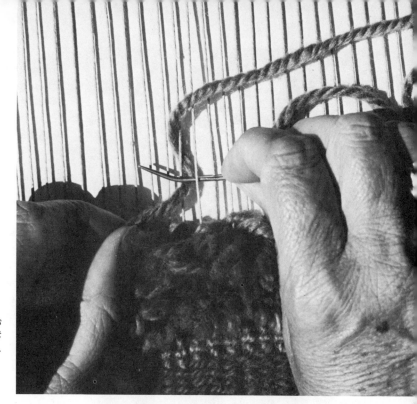

46. Ghiordes knot—detail shows how to weave it and where to cut it to achieve a fuzzy texture.

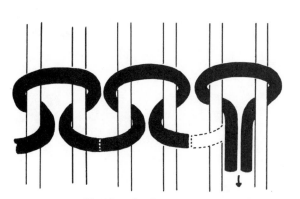

47. Ghiordes knot as used in sampler—after the three rows of Egyptian knots that closed the tops of the seven slits.

48. Almond motif close-up shows how you can push weft apart and weave in a new color.

49. French knots add textural interest in areas that seem too flat.

only a little room remains on your sampler. Finish the space at the top with plain weave. When it is done, you might decide that you would enjoy a color change in certain spots. It's never too late! Just pull the weft apart, using both hands, some of it up, some of it down, to reveal bare warp in an almond shape. Thread your needle with a contrasting color and fill in these shapes with plain weave (Plate 48). The almond shapes are an excellent way to introduce darks into light areas and lights into dark areas. As you study the photographs in this book, you will see how many of our weavers employ the almond shape to break up space. If an area seems too large with nothing happening in it, you can always add almonds, even after every other part is finished.

REMOVING SAMPLER FROM LOOM

With a crochet hook, gently lift the loops out of the slits on the back of the loom. You can push the weaving out to occupy these little loops at the ends. Sometimes weavers tie fringe into the loops at the bottom of the tapestry. I did not do that, but the medallion needed more embellishment, so I added French knots (Plate 49).

5

After the Sampler...
Variations and Elaborations

Now that your own sampler is finished, you are ready to understand and enjoy the devices our weavers use in their work.

Study Jean Robinson's circular hanging which she wove on embroidery hoops instead of a cardboard loom (Plate 50, Color Plate 3). Inspired by a Tamayo painting, she chose soft colors: gold, rose, a muted earthy orange, green, turquoise, and then (it comes as a surprise) a touch of lavender. She warped the weaving on the smaller hoop, first with bands going in one direction. She planned her tapestry slits and did the weaving. Then she warped the bands going in the opposite direction through the tapestry slits in the first bands. The bands of weaving actually weave with each other. When the weaving was finished, Jean snapped the large hoop over the smaller one and tied the wrapped and twisted hanging yarns in place.

Notice that not all the slits were used for crossing warp. The open slit is in itself decorative. It does not have to do anything except *be* there. Jean worked for interesting divisions of

space, both in the bands and in the areas between the bands. As you think to yourself whether spaces seem interesting or dull, you will grow sensitive to design.

We show detail photographs from large weavings to give you a feeling for the design properties our weavers discover in the materials they choose and develop further by the techniques they use (Plates 51 and 52). Notice how their wefts meander freely, making curves and almonds; how they vary plain weave to show warp threads, compressing it or loosening it, adding knots and loops to get more texture. Do the wrapped warps intrigue you? You will find this device explained in Drawing 83.

Most tapestry experts seem to agree that the arrangement of light and dark areas is more important than the colors chosen for the work, and that the proportion of colors in relation to one another is most important. Usually fewer colors are used than appear in a painting. The emphasis is on changes of texture within a color —a number of whites of different weights in a

51. *Detail from a large weaving by Arvella Durham shows the effective texturing you can get by combining cut loops (Ghiordes knot), plain weave firmly woven, plain weave with warp showing, plain weave with several threads used as one, Egyptian knot and embroidered French knots.*

52. *Detail from Sharon Berg's weaving shows the variety of texture you get by changing the compactness of weaving. Much of the tactile beauty of tapestry is a revel in the threadiness of thread, the wooliness of yarn, the stubbornness of jute, the softness of silk.*

white area, a number of blues of different weights in a blue area, and so on. Very limited color schemes seem the most effective — three colors, or perhaps five being quite enough for one weaving, using several variations of tone in each color.

If the warp shows at all, and if it is dark, it has a harmonizing effect on whatever color scheme is chosen. Colors that might seem to clash or be too strident when placed side by side are often compatible with the neutralizing effect of a dark warp to harmonize them. Conversely, colors that seem pleasant together before they are woven often appear drab and dull or uninteresting after they are woven. The only way to determine what is good together is to try it; weave a sample of the colors you contemplate using.

50. *Circular wall hanging 20" in diameter by Jean Robinson. Bands with tapestry slits are woven directly onto wooden embroidery hoops which then become the permanent frame.*

53. *Tapestry vest by Dr. Charles Stevens uses tapestry and staggered slits to expose a mauve lining behind the design done in several tones of green, from light to dark.*

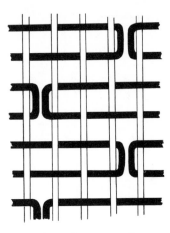

54. *Staggered tapestry slit.*

55. *Variation of staggered tapestry slit. These slits can be made to have a stair-step effect by weaving over the warp more than once before moving the slit to a new position.*

HATCHING

The method of moving from light to dark or from one color into another gradually is called hatching. Simple hatching is best understood by half-closing one's eyes and squinting at a printed column in a newspaper. The change of tone from solidly printed lines to lines that only partly cross the column is the principle involved in hatching.

In simple hatching, the lines of light yarn run parallel to the dark that they penetrate (Plate 57). In more complicated hatching, triangles of light color may be built up in the dark areas (Plates 58 and 59).

Almost everyone has favorite colors, colors to which he responds in a positive way. Starting with those colors you can gradually, through observation, extend the palette of your likes. Look at fabrics and objects in nature long enough to describe each color in words. The artist Van Gogh had remarkable skill not only in mixing colors in paint, but in observing color in nature and then describing it. We can read his published letters and know that when he looked at an old loom, he saw not just old wood but "greenish browned oak." His vision was precise. Our own becomes more precise as we work at making it so.

The most important thing about color is to enjoy it. Watch what happens when you weave a bright red yarn into orange or magenta warp. How different it looks when you change the warp to hot pink. Each color changes every other color, not only by weaving into the other but also by being near it. Watching these color changes and reacting to the change is an enjoyable way to extend your color sensitivity.

Dr. Charles Stevens produced an interesting effect by introducing a surprise color for the lining of his vest (Plate 53). You don't expect to see a low-key violet under the mossy green

56. Fur parka, tasseled feet, flapping arms are whimsical embellishments for stylized doll woven of white wool with brown symbol lock-stitched on its chest.

57. *Simple hatching, in which lines of one color of yarn run parallel to the color they penetrate to effect a color change.*

58. *Another example of hatching, more complicated, showing how triangles of colors are built up in block of another color.*

59. *Detail of an extremely intricate example of hatching, from Doris Fox's weaving (Plate 89).*

yarns. But when you see it, you are glad it is there.

A vest may seem quite a large undertaking to the beginning weaver, but it is actually very simple and easy to do. Dr. Stevens cut looms to match a vest pattern and warped them from top to bottom just the way you warped your sampler — the difference being that some of the warps end at the armholes He used plain weave and tapestry slits; the open slits allow the mauve lining to show through.

Yarn in this weaving changes from one tone

of green to another in the pattern of points, re-peated on vest back, too. This is done by weaving staggered tapestry slits (Drawings 54 and 55). You can stagger slits in each woven row as diagramed, or arrange them in stairsteps, as Dr. Stevens did; that is, by weaving not just one but several rows of weft before the slit moves to the new position.

In your sampler, you practiced locked slits, so you know how Beverly Nemetz wove the design into the body of her Eskimo Pillow Doll (Plate 56). The fur, the tassels, the design and the humor of the long, flat arms are interesting enough without adding complicated weaves or knots. Made to be hung as a mobile, the doll is done entirely with plain weave and locked slits. The head is a wrapped hoop, circled with fur.

Your sampler also taught you the Egyptian knot, which you will recognize as the rib in the background of the Virgo panel by Jo Dendel (Plate 60).

60. "Virgo" by Jo Dendel. One of 12 zodiac panels measuring 16″ across top, 14″ high. Egyptian knot gives background a ribbed effect; facial features are outlined with a couching stitch.

*61. Detail of intricate laid-in design
used in a handwoven African blanket.
Collection of Mr. and Mrs. Jo Dendel.*

6

More Techniques,
More Things to Make

A sampler is not quite big enough for you to learn all the useful tapestry techniques, so we suggest two more small projects: a pocket and a purse, both useful. The pocket is planned to give you confidence in doing a meandering weft. The purse will acquaint you with laid-in design.

MEANDERING WEFT

It takes more courage than most beginners have to start a large project with the weaving thread wandering at whim through the warps. But a little pocket, freely done, will show you how exciting this freedom can be. Rosita Montgomery started the pocket we picture without any sketch or any previous idea of what she might do. She simply selected some colors that would harmonize with a brown dress of coarse weave. Using the darkest weft, she ran it around through the warps (Plate 62), pushing it here, pulling it there, using the needle to slide the wefts somewhere else until the area seemed to be designed to please her. One can develop great sensitivity to design just by pushing a meandering weft around in an area, watching what happens, and reacting to it. If it "feels right", it probably is. The weaving continues, in freely meandering fashion, within the pre-liminary outlines—a pleasing collection of textures and colors (Plates 63 and 64).

Instead of meandering freely, the weft thread may meander according to a plan. You can develop exciting texture if the weaving thread goes forward, turns back on itself for a space, turns and goes forward as before (Drawing 65, Plate 66).

LAID-IN DESIGN

A handsome and easy way to decorate plain weave is to add a contrasting yarn, laid in alongside the weaving thread. You may put the contrasting yarn in your needle along with the weaving thread and weave them in together. Or you may do the plain weaving first, darning in the contrasting color later. I wove a small purse with an orange rectangle on a field of green yarn; then came back to make a simple design of laid-in green yarn, following the ins and outs of the plain weave every fourth row in the orange rectangle. (Plate 67).

The five straight rows in the orange rectangle illustrate the simplest possible design using the laid-in device. African weavers make intricate and complicated use of it, as shown in the blanket we brought back from the West Coast of Africa (Plate 61).

62. Pocket loom 5x7" by Rosita Montgomery
is warped with double strands of mohair
yarn. The warp is separated by the two rows
of chain stitch top and bottom so that in
effect you have a loom warped ⅛" apart
instead of ¼". Rosita weaves her design by
using the darkest yarn first.

63. Finished pocket has the dark
outlines filled in with a pleasing
collection of colors and textures.

64. Pocket detail shows the variety of yarns
and weaves used for fill-ins: plain weave,
Egyptian knot, fine yarns, medium yarns and
sometimes two colors in the needle at once.

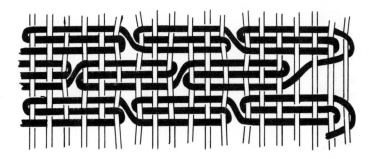

65. Detail showing a
planned meandering weft.

66. Planned meandering weft as it
looks on a loom—using double
yarn (top) and single strand (below).

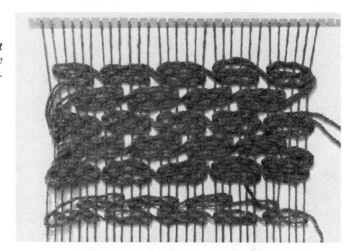

I am so intrigued with the simplicity and the possibilities of laid-in design that I plan to explore it more deeply. For example, if one wishes to introduce beads into a weaving, this is a good way to do it (Plate 68). Simply string a bead on the contrasting thread each time it surfaces. When you weave the thread back under the warp, the bead is secured. Another idea: Make a knot in the contrasting thread each time it surfaces (Plate 69). This surface design of knots is a good starting point for future experiments.

THE ECCENTRIC WEFT

In tapestry from many parts of the world, we find weaving threads that are not at right angles to the warp. Rosita Montgomery wove a pocket to experiment with this in a small way. When the unusual, or eccentric wefts as we call them, are quite noticeably eccentric and are tightly woven, small bulges appear on the surface. Because of this, the tapestry actually assumes a vaguely sculptured appearance. Tapestries from Egypt woven by the children of Harrania are a good example of this.

The picture we show (Plate 70) is a detail from a tapestry in the collection of Dr. and Mrs. William Wagner. The Wagners visited Harrania (a village near the Pyramids) and talked to Prof. Ramses Wissa Wassef, under whose direction the children work, weaving on simple wood frames. Nothing is drawn or designed in advance. The children simply create in a joyful, spontaneous way.

49

67. *Laid-in design: one row of background color is woven over every 4th row of color block. Ends of yarn are knotted for added decorative effect.*

Those who would like to read more about the project at Harrania will enjoy a book by the Forman brothers, they won the confidence of Professor Wassef and wrote a beautiful book: *Tapestries from Egypt.*

It is interesting that these glowing tapestries are now being woven within sight of the Pyramids in the very country where the ancient Copts wove the garments we study with close attention and gratitude today.

EARLY WEAVERS

The Copts were the early Christians of Egypt. We would know little about them had they not left a record of their culture in their graves. By the end of the third century most of Egypt had been Christianized. The Roman Empire was falling apart in the West. Out in the provinces and in monastic centers far from the great cities at the mouth of the Nile, the Copts de-

68. *Laid-in design of beads—as you weave over and under (plain weave) with contrasting yarn, add a bead each time needle surfaces.*

69. *Laid-in design of knots—same as for beads except you make a knot each time needle surfaces.*

veloped a truly individual and great art style. Many of their woven garments have influenced the vestments still in use in Christian churches today.

The Copts embalmed their dead. They dressed the body in linen and placed it on a wooden board with a pillow under the head, and buried it in the hot desert sands of Egypt. Spindles have been found in women's graves, weaving utensils and tools in men's graves. This division of labor—women spinning and men weaving— is the custom in much of West Africa today.

Making great use of Bible stories and the symbolism of their Christian religion, the Copts wove bands and medallions for their tunics. In their medallions, the amount of area to be filled determined the size of a figure; natural proportions gave way to design considerations. Perhaps that is why these compositions have an arresting charm. They surely do inspire contemporary weavers.

Discovering the Copts and the art they produced is just one of the serendipitous benefits of learning to weave, made all the more pleasurable because it is so unexpected.

An interest in weaving may also lead one deeply into the culture of our own Navajo Indians. Or into the lives and hearts of tribal Africa, as it did me. Peruvian tapestries from gravesites leave us incredulous; we get out a magnifying glass and try to understand their intricacies and technical skills. Some of these were made before the Spanish Conquest, even before the Incas came to southern and central Peru. We see vegetable colorings that glow after having been buried in the sands for two thousand years. We smell in the fibers the smoke from embalming fires lighted centuries ago.

One can travel back and forth through the centuries, and from continent to continent, making discoveries. And learning ever more about weaving.

70. Detail of a tapestry woven by children of Harrania, Egypt— an excellent example of the eccentric weft used in freehand design. Collection of Dr. and Mrs. William Wagner.

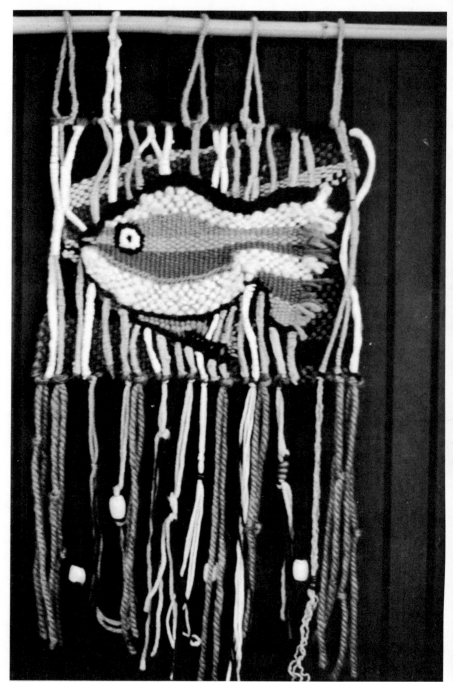

71."Sun Fish" tapestry,
12x26", by Lisa Bannies.
Woven on a loom that has been
warped on both sides—fish is
woven in front, waves in back.

7
Warping for Special Effects

So far we have been dealing with warps that lie parallel to one another and cover only the face of the loom. There are other ways to warp and some of them are very exciting. Suppose you want to make a seamless tube for a pillow or purse. You begin by cutting some hardboard for the project and notching both ends; these will be the top and bottom of your pillow or purse.

WARPING FRONT AND BACK OF LOOM

Our interesting problem is how to warp this without having the loom imprisoned in the finished work. The way out of weaving oneself into a corner is to warp the face of the loom just as you did for the sampler. Then turn the loom over and warp the back in the same way. The weft yarns go around and around the loom, front to back to front again, making a seamless tube. When the warps are lifted out of their notches on both ends of the loom, the loom slides right out the end. Do an oval shape the same way except be prepared to bend and break the cardboard to get it out of the opening, which will be smaller than the opening in a rectangle.

To get the effect of a two-level tapestry, you can warp both sides of the loom and weave them differently, instead of going around and around with the same pattern and weaving thread. In her little "Fish" tapestry, Lisa Bannies wove the back warp in a wave-like pattern to suggest the sea (Plate 71, Color Plate 5). The colors are ocean colors. On the front of the loom she wove the fish in the central area, and tightly wrapped the warps above and below the fish (see drawing 83). When she removed the loom, the ocean pattern behind the fish shows through the wrapped warps. Note that the side of the ocean on view is actually the wrong side of the fabric as it was woven on the back of the loom, so the weaver must be careful not to push any loose ends through to what seems to be the back but will really be the front of the work.

ECCENTRIC WARPING

We have talked about eccentric wefts and now we will see that warps can be eccentric, too, with interesting effects.

One begins an eccentric warp by crossing the central area of the loom instead of starting along one side. It follows a pattern: After leading the warp across the cardboard and through a slit to the back, you bring the second warp up through the slit to the *right* of the first warp. Then take it across the loom and down through the slit to the *left* of the starting warp. In other words, the warps cross on the face of the cardboard. Continue in this manner until the loom is warped. You'll have a considerable pile-up

*72. Dodecagon (12-sided) loom, 36"
across, by Jo Dendel—with weaving
just started. Eccentric warps build
up in center and are left exposed.*

where the warps cross; they are too close together to be woven, and need not be—they're
interesting just the way they are. They give an
extra dimension to the work. In Plate 72, you
see how Jo Dendel warped a twelve-sided hardboard loom with the eccentric warp crossing the
center.

But eccentric warp does not need to cross in
the center. The work can be planned so that
several of these warp build-ups take place in
various areas of the loom. For ease of work, the
bottom layer should be woven before the next
layer of warp is strung out over it. See if you can
find bottom among the warp crossings on Bici
Linklater's loom (Plate 73).

Sometimes only part of a circle or rectangle
is warped on the loom. Additional warps are
anchored in the warp threads already on the
loom and these take dynamic diagonal directions. You can see this in Jean Robinson's weav-

ing, which she calls "Winter." It is woven in
Christmasy metallic threads (Plate 74).

WARPING SPECIAL SHAPES

If a weaving is not to be the same size on
both edges, the difference can be managed by
varying the spacing of the warp. Jo Dendel's
loom in Plate 72 is sixteen inches along the top
and ten inches at the bottom. The notches are
of necessity closer together at the bottom. By
starting at the center, one can usually adjust
the difference by eye, but it could be mathe-
matically calculated. The loom is warped with
two threads in each notch in order to have extra
threads with which to work in the parts of the
design requiring detail (Plate 75).

Weaving collars and yokes presents this same
problem of spacing the warp because the distance around the neck is less than the distance
around the outer edge. In collars, the direction

73. "Crossing Paths", 14" square, by Bici Linklater. Eccentric warp runs diagonally from side to side as well as top to bottom. Strips are built up by weaving one layer before warping the next.
When finished, the weaving will be appliquéd on a pillow.

74. "Winter", 12" diameter, by Jean Robinson. Only scattered warp threads are attached to the wire circle—additional warps anchored to warps already there produce dynamic line movement within the circle.

of the warp changes with the structure. You can see (Plate 76) how Helen Hennessey marks a collar loom with ruled lines to show warp directions and spacing, prior to warping it. She worked it in rather fine yarns in a vivid blending of hot pinks, oranges and reds, with beads in the same colors (Plate 77, Color Plate 15).

You can form points by bringing the warps closer together toward the ends and also by weaving over two or more warps as though they were one. To make rays for a sun I wove, I warped a circular loom with eccentric warping, threads crossing in the center, and just

75. *"Gemini" loom by Jo Dendel shows how to warp a trapezoid— there are the same number of slits top and bottom, but those at the bottom are closer together.*

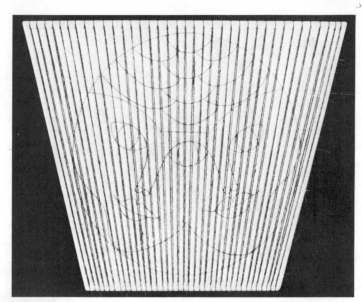

76. *Cardboard loom (below) for collar has been ruled to show notching and to show direction and spacing for warp threads.*

77. *Finished collar (below, right) by Helen Hennessey is vibrant— Egyptian knots and laid-in beads are in purples, reds, pinks, oranges, greens and blues.*

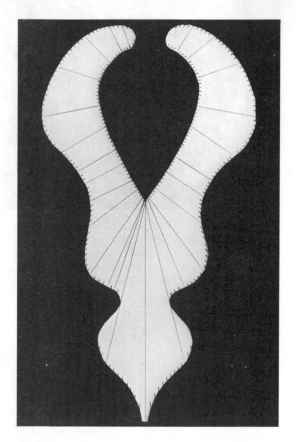

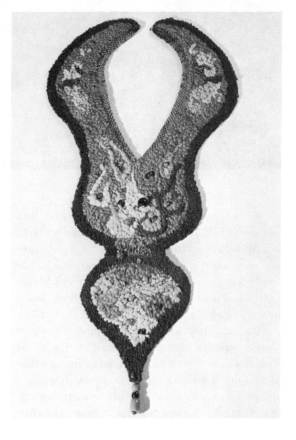

enough of them to get the width of the ray. Then I wove it from the outside edge to the center where the warps cross. The warp that continues on across the loom is not woven—instead, it's tied in a knot to make a tassel (Plate 78). When all the rays were woven, they were sewed to the perimeter of the sun.

Sometimes when a piece of work is to have considerable detail, one needs extra warps. The detailed area, a face for instance, can be woven on a separate small loom with twice as many warps as the larger area. The face in Plate 79 will be woven as sketched, removed from the cardboard and incorporated into a large tapestry. It is attached by pulling the warps of the large weaving, one at a time, through every other interval in the more densely warped piece.

Eva Fedorchek warped some correspondence cards with eccentric warp and the warp itself was so interesting that she did not need to weave into it. Each card is different as she rearranges the warping pattern (Plate 81).

Elizabeth Bennett wrapped three hoops of different sizes and fastened them together. The warps go in different directions in order to give variety to the finished weaving which will be done in bright colors (Plate 80).

Extra warps are often added and wrapped for textural effects. Plate 82 shows a band for a sleeve woven in white wool by Roméo Reyna. It is to be applied to a black dress. The added warps are long enough to twist and curl. They are secured by adding them to the warps in the woven area and weaving over both yarns as though they were one.

79. Warping for face loom is half-spaced—closer weaving gives better detail. Woven face is then transferred to a larger tapestry.

78. Detail from wall hanging by Sharon Berg shows points formed by bringing warps closer at ends, weaving and then knotting them together.

80. *"Hoopla" by Elizabeth Bennett is a wall decoration with three hoops—warped in different directions. Weft yarns will be in reds, pinks and oranges.*

81. *Correspondence cards with eccentric warping by Eva Fedorchek are interesting with no further weaving.*

THE YARN WRAPPING TECHNIQUE

Wrapped yarns give a distinctive effect, not otherwise obtainable. Wrapped yarns seem controlled, yet free. They are an easy way to introduce a Joseph's-coat-of-colors effect. Wrapping a thread makes it seem more important.

You may wrap warps simply by going around and around with a separate yarn. Catch the beginning of this yarn under the first few wrappings, and when you finish, work the end back under the wrapped area with a needle.

A somewhat easier way to secure the end of the wrapping yarn is to take a separate piece of yarn or thread and form a loop. Use the loop to anchor the wrapping yarn (Drawing 83). You may use thread of a different color for this —it is easier to find and pull out when its job is done. Run the loop from the bottom of the area to be wrapped to a point a little above where you want to stop wrapping. Wrap both warp and loop together, around and around up to the loop. Thread the end of the wrapping thread through the loop and pull it down into the body of the wrapped area by pulling the two ends of the loop from the bottom. Snip off the pulling ends of the thread close to the wrapping, or pull the thread out. We learned this technique from fishermen who use wrapping to prepare their gear.

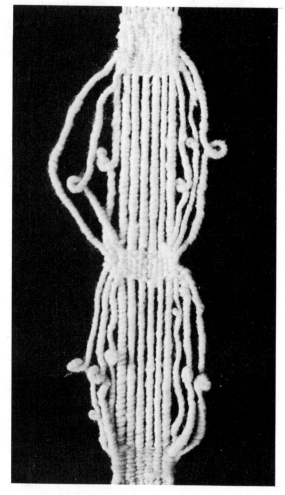

82. Sleeve band by Roméo Reyna has added warps that have been wrapped to give them more importance.

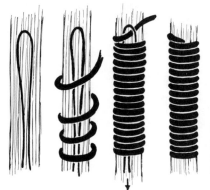

83. Detail of wrapping technique—to secure end of wrapping yarn, form a loop of contrasting thread and wrap yarn as shown, then pull yarn end into wrapped area.

84. Collection of mandalas shows the many interpretations artists
give to the symbol of the sun. Woven by Frances Schroeder,
Jean Robinson, Helen Dickey, Helen Trescott, Louanne Matsler.

8
Weaving a Mandala

The sun, which "like a strong man runs its course with joy", is probably the inspiration for more great design than any other natural object. Sometimes circular designs represent the actual sun. At other times, a circle may be a symbol of the earth, the full moon, a bird's nest, eternity. Carl G. Jung, the famous Swiss psychologist, called our attention to *mandala,* a Sanskrit word meaning a magic circle.

Dr. Jung saw the mandala as a symbol of the harmonious relationship of a man with his Self. In his book, *Man and His Symbols,* he notes many examples from many cultures. He shows us a Navajo sand painter making a mandala in a ritual healing. After the patient has circled the mandala, he must sit inside it. In far-separated cultures, people contemplate a mandala to restore wholeness of the spirit and to achieve inner harmony.

Someone has pointed out that when children play joyful, peaceful games, they form themselves into a mandala. There are the singing games done in a circle, the Maypole dance,

many folk dances. Aggressive games such as "Crack the Whip" are more likely to take the form of a straight line.

Mandalas appear in children's drawings from all over the world, and if a child is left to himself without guidance about what he shall draw, he will sooner or later come up with a mandala. This, then, must be a symbol of universal attraction. It has been said that man does not invent symbols; he *discovers* them. The search to discover leads to interesting patterns of thought and to art that has more than surface meaning.

One of the best ways to contemplate a mandala is to weave one. Sometimes the weaving is done on cardboard and then transferred to a wire ring or an embroidery hoop; sometimes the hoop or ring is wrapped with yarn and the warping and weaving is done directly inside the circle. We have gathered some of the mandalas done by our group of weavers to show the variety possible within the confines of a circle (Plate 84, Color Plate 1).

85. *Nine mandalas woven by Judy Whelan for a walnut screen designed by Jo Dendel. Designs are unified by using the same colors for all.*

Jean Robinson wove a mandala for each of the four seasons. *Autumn* is a circle bound by braided cornhusks and done in the colors of turning leaves. *Winter* is in Christmas gold. *Spring* is as delicate as new leaves and fresh shoots of bulbs and grass. *Summer* looks as hearty as a vegetable harvest—the greens of peppers and peas, the reds of ripe tomatoes. As the seasons wheel into time, she takes the appropriate mandala out of storage and hangs it to mark the event.

Nine mandalas woven by Judy Whelan on 18-inch wire hoops were set into walnut frames, to make a folding screen for her husband's of-

fice. The screen itself was designed and made by Jo Dendel (Plate 85, Color Plate 11). The same vivid wool colors run through all of the mandalas, but each one is a unique expression of the weaver's skill and imagination.

Virginia Weeks' oval-shaped mandala was woven on notched oval cardboard. She positioned the finished weaving, still on its loom, inside a large wooden hoop and anchored it to the hoop with yarn laced through the mandala's warping loops, then removed the cardboard (Plate 86, Color Plate 8). The same device, but with entirely different effect, was used by Louella Ballerino (Plate 87, Color Plate

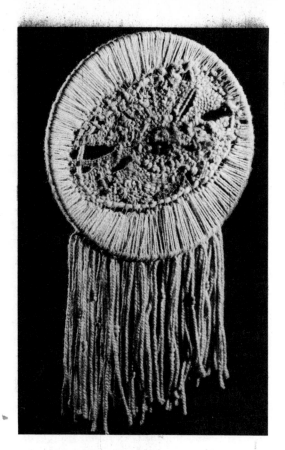

86. Oval mandala by Virginia Weeks is warped into a round ring with yarn—no further weaving. Beads are added to the fringe for interest.

87. Round mandala by Louella Ballerino, warped and woven in an open cross and square pattern, is set into a larger ring with radiant warping. Rays are woven, and gossamer threads strung with beads are tied here and there.

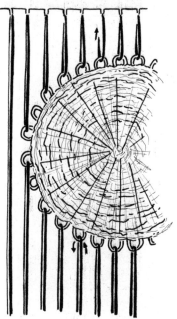

88. Detail showing how a mandala is warped to the loom for the second stage—weaving around it. Warp is threaded into the loops before the mandala is removed from its own cardboard loom.

7). Virginia's weaving is solid, textured with coarse yarn; Louella's is as ethereal as gossamer beaded with raindrops. Both are delightful.

A mandala may be thought of and hung as a completed weaving. Or it may become the focal point and center of interest of a larger creation.

Why not weave the mandala into a larger tapestry in the first place, instead of transferring it from a small cardboard to a larger loom? This is often done. But there are at least two advantages in making the small weavings first and later doing something further with them. First, this gives the weaver a beginning, something to work around. There is something rather frightening about a large blank set of warps. It is a little like a blank sheet of white paper that a writer knows he must fill. Writing anything, just anything, to get rid of the appalling blankness of that rectangle of paper is a help. The small weavings, set into the warps of a big loom, help you get started.

The second advantage of weaving these centers of interest first is that the warp in the small weavings may go "any which way" (eccentric warping), giving additional design interest.

The first step in bringing the small mandala into a larger weaving is to decide on the size of the larger statement and prepare a cardboard or piece of masonite with notches to receive the warp. Before beginning to warp, it is a good idea to place this loom on a table top where you will walk by it several times a day. Arrange the small weaving or weavings (still on their looms) where they seem right to you. Each time you pass the arrangement you have made, study the position of the mandalas. Move them a little this way or that. React to the new positionings. The most satisfactory designs come about if you, the designer, have been willing to indulge your inborn passion for arranging. When the locations feel right to you, mark their positions on the loom.

Begin warping as you did for your sampler. When you come to one of the mandalas, thread the free end of the warp through a needle, bring it into the back of the mandala's cardboard circle, threading it through the little stitch-like showings of warp (Drawing 88). Sometimes you will not know which loop of warp to secure, but it does not matter very much so long as the warps on the larger loom keep running close

89. Wall hanging by Doris Fox shows how the mandala blends into a larger weaving in waves of color using the hatching technique (Chapter 5).

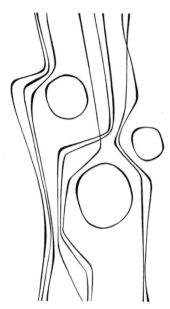

90. *Variation on pillow design #92 shows repeat of elements to make a rectangular tapestry.*

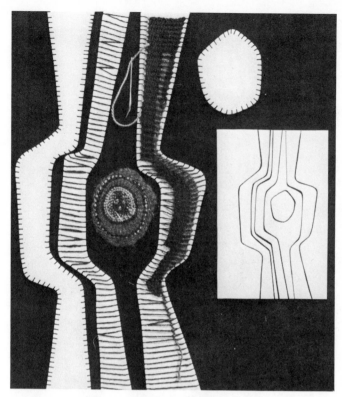

92. *Tapestry appliqué for a pillow top by Jean Stange shows design plan, finished mandala and cardboard looms with work in progress.*

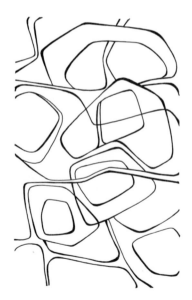

91. *In another variation the mandalas are repeated in clusters, in small, medium and large sizes.*

to parallel, one with the next. If a long length of warp tends to snarl, do not hesitate to cut it to a convenient length and then tie a knot in it when you have need for more. The knot will be embedded in the finished weaving and will not show. Some notches on each side of the circle will not be used at all, but this does not matter; the weft threads will weave into and secure these. Remove cardboard from mandala after warp from the larger panel comes into the warp of the mandala.

After ensnaring the principal design area or areas (the mandalas) into the total area, the next design problem is to draw some lines that will relate these shapes into a total compo-

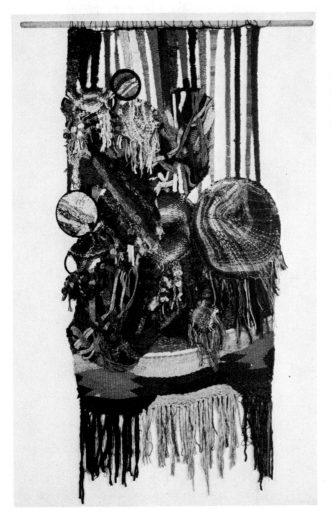

93. *Award-winning tapestry by Tess Goldsmith combines mandalas with intertwined woven strips and fringe in a fantastically complicated weaving that started with three embroidery hoops.*

sition. Our group felt that Doris Fox was unusually successful in solving this problem (Plate 89). Her weaving is in mossy greens, burnt oranges, browns and white. As she moved from one color to the next, she used the tapestry device known as *hatching*.

Jean Stange grouped one mandala shape with three linear shapes of varying widths. These were woven, each on its own loom, then the shapes were sewed to textured neutral linen to make a pillow top (Plate 92). Jean later thought of using the same looms to repeat the design in other colors for the opposite side of the pillow.

Next, her explorations led to the use of three mandala shapes, each a different size, combined with lines that utilize the total area of a large rectangular weaving. Subtleties of shading and color changes will be worked out on the loom. Experience shows that tapestries that hold to-

94. *Individual squares from the screen in Plate 85 used as wall decoration—a good solution if you like the idea of walnut-framed mandalas but you have no use for a screen.*

gether visually, from a design standpoint, have some large sweeping lines that cross most of the area (Drawing 90).

Jean's third experiment led to the clustering of mandala shapes, again of varying sizes (Drawing 91). If a shape is repeated, or nearly repeated, in small, medium and large proportions, it sets up a rhythm—a progression of size intervals. Having all the shapes in a composition the same size is a little like music written entirely in whole notes. The monotony of such a song may be soothing, but soon we are lulled to sleep, or we're longing for some excitement —a change of pace.

Another thing we experience in Jean's designs is the satisfaction of the bent line. A bent line is a curve that is straight for part of its length. It is a good design line because it combines the grace of the curve with the strength of a straight line. It is particularly good in these three designs because the designer employs it to reconcile the curves of the mandalas to the rectangles of the tapestries.

To see how an artist develops a complex tapestry, look at Tess Goldsmith's hanging that grew from three embroidery hoops (Plate 93, Color Plate 13). She wrapped the three hoops, each a different size, and warped and wove each one differently. She then warped a large frame with dark warp and distributed the hoops within the area. Since the weaving would be quite large, more circles seemed necessary. These were woven and added. Slender woven strips came next, playfully interweaving with other woven strips. Finally, the entire warp expanse was brought together, woven with triangular color transitions at the bottom of the hanging. The colors are rich reds, pinks, mustards and golds. This hanging is an award-winning tapestry. As one approaches it, the awesome overall effect gives way to a desire in the beholder to examine each intricacy, each texture, each wrapping of yarn.

68

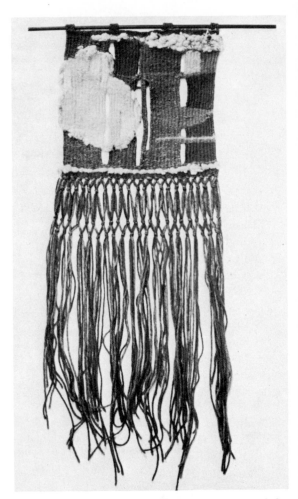

95. A desert stone inspired this small tapestry by Louella Ballerino. Extra yarns are tied into warp to make the long fringe (Chapter 10).

9

Where Design Ideas
Come From

If, as you worked on your sampler, you found pleasure in manipulating the yarn, if you felt a tingle of exultation, no matter how faint, you've known the first stir of something that may become very important to you. It may completely change your life.

That great thinker, Martin Buber, has told us that we may treat things, other persons, and even ourselves, either as an "it" or as a "Thou". A Thou feeling of respect toward the universe is the hallmark of the craftsman. This does not mean that he "just loves everything". In fact, he is highly discriminating. He can have Thou feelings only toward that which is honestly itself. He cannot relate to the tawdry, the sham or the show-off. Elegance is sometimes an offense. The thread from an old potato sack may have more appeal for him than cords that glitter and shine. It is more earthy and closer to its source.

We have in our time become alienated from the earth. Jute, wool and sisal, puffs of unbleached cotton, driftwood and shells and pebbles, sea-polished glass and bleached bones, a seed pod, a weathered barn board, a bright feather dropped from a bird in flight—these are a few of the offerings from earth. We are free to ignore or accept. But we need to cultivate a friendship with earth and what it offers.

When I was a child growing up on an Iowa farm, I did not think old potato sacks or unpainted barn boards or milkweed pods were beautiful. My mother said they were, but I thought she was just clutching at something to be glad about; that was her nature. To me, the potato sacks suggested back-breaking stoop labor in the fields. Weed pods were from plants that should have been hoed out before they set seed. Unpainted barn boards were a constant reminder that money was short and that shoes for school in the fall after a barefoot summer were more important than paint for the barn.

It was only when I came back to these familiar things after having lived with the tribespeople of West Africa who revere the earth as their Great Mother, that I realized what my

96. *Photograph of dried salt and mud forms suggests design lines and colors for a weaving.*

97. *Weaving in process: In a free translation of her photograph, Joan Coverdale improvises with yarn textures and colors—even with seaweed.*

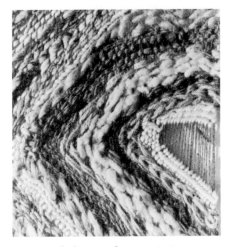

98. *Detail showing how variations in color, yarn texture and weave interpret dried salt and mud forms.*

99. *Heavily textured weaving by Phil Freeman employs the symbols of Cross and circle. Red and orange yarns are used together in loops for intense color effect. Weights at bottom are stoneware medallions.*

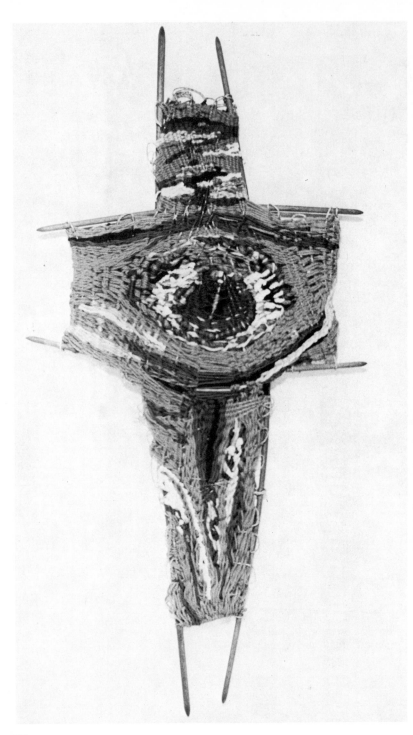

100. Freely but also intricately woven Cross by Jean Freeman stands 4½ feet tall. Both warps and wefts meander freely, crossing every which way. Colors are appropriate to an adobe church: purples, reds, greens and white. The four crossed sticks were pushed through warping loops (but not through all of them) when the weaving was finished.

own mother had been wise enough to know all the time. Perhaps my friendship and feeling for these earth things is firmer and deeper because I came back to it from half the world away. And this is why sticks and stones and bones find their way into my work.

DESIGNS IN NATURE

Sometimes a certain stone is not physically attached or embedded in a tapestry but the contemplation of the stone suggests the color and design of the tapestry. A stone picked up in a California desert provided Louella Ballerino with all the impetus she needed to do a splendid little tapestry. She did not try to copy the stone, but to interpret it (Plate 95, Color Plate 4).

What next? A walk on the beach or along a meandering stream. A time of browsing through meadows and woods. Chase some shadows as they change with the breeze and the light. Study the pattern of bark on a tree, the whirl of eddying water in a pool.

PHOTOGRAPHS

Color photography has relieved the artist of the need to show how things actually look. The artist's new duty is to help us know the feeling aroused by a beautiful object in nature. A tapestry does not need to represent precisely any scene or object. It may come closer to nature if it does not. One design device which many

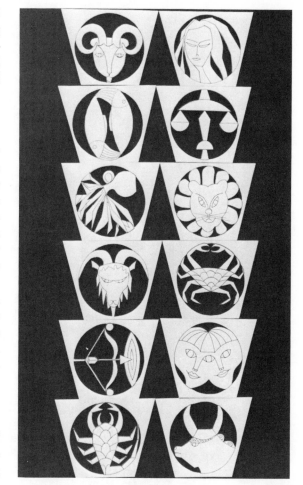

101. Zodiac signs by Jo Dendel. Background will be done in Egyptian knot, circular designs in plain weave outlined with the couching stitch.

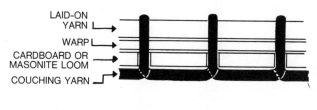

LAID-ON YARN
WARP
CARDBOARD OR MASONITE LOOM
COUCHING YARN

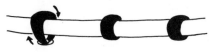

102. Couching stitch: detail shows how masonite is drilled following circular line so a couching thread can be wrapped from back of loom around warp and laid-on yarn. The laid-on yarn defines the circle, separates it from background.

73

103. *Child's drawing duplicated in weaving by Celia Wagner on a loom warped horizontally. White halo effect around the figure is a device the weaver admired in a Polish tapestry.*

104. Polish tapestry detail (from the Allen-Related Art Dept. collection owned by the University of Wisconsin) shows figure separated from background by halo effect.

75

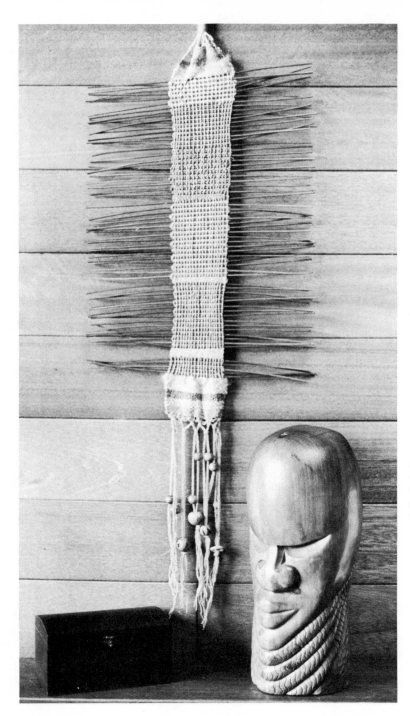

105. Like many weavers, Helen Dickey uses yarns to enmesh and display found things. Here she has subordinated the yarns to emphasize the twigs.

artists find useful is to project slides of scenes they have photographed. Turn them out of focus until the literal subject matter disappears and only the colors and shapes, the dark and light patternings remain. Photographs of autumn color, of ocean tide pools, of sunsets and many other natural beauties lend themselves to this treatment. This is a sort of distillation of the poetry in scenes that have moved us.

Joan Coverdale is interested in the sea life and birds of our Newport Bay. She photographed an area that she calls "Dried Salt and Mud Forms" (Plate 96). Not as a copy of her photograph, but using it as an inspiration, she repeated some of the shapes and shadings in her tapestry (Plates 97 and 98). The tapestry is in the colors of salt and sand and she has used some seaweed in the weaving along with jute and yarn. Seaweed gets very stiff and unwieldy when it is dry but if it is left out in the dew overnight, it becomes pliable again and can be threaded in a needle.

SYMBOLS

Symbols produce in us feelings and moods that bypass language; indeed, symbols have no need of words. At the time the great cathedrals were built in Europe, Christian symbolism was a language which even the illiterate understood. In secular as well as in religious life, bright banners were everywhere. Flags waved at jousts and fluttered from gay tents. Knights had their own colors and during the Crusades, they carried the symbol of the Cross to faraway lands.

The bright red tapestry by Phil Freeman with its symbols of Cross and circle (Plate 99), seems to have come right out of those vigorous times. The stately medallions of stone he used for weights on the bottom echo the theme of the weaving. The entire effect is achieved through change of textures in the red and orange yarns which in the loops are used together as one.

106. A white tapestry on brown warps by Helen Hennessey traces the curves of two tree branches. After weaving, warps from rectangular loom were pulled through holes drilled in branches. The weaving is an outstanding example of improvisation within the boundaries of the branches.

107. Tearing up paper and arranging it often suggests a design idea. To Mr. and Mrs. Roger Dunn these shapes looked like the Rocky Mountains as seen from a jet plane. They paper-clipped torn papers to warps and have started to outline them for a 4x6' wall hanging that will be worked in mountain colors.

The Cross, woven by Jean Freeman and mounted on four crossed sticks, is in purples and reds and greens and white. It seems to belong in an adobe church in the American southwest and would add warmth as well as meaning to the wall (Plate 100). The rough textures, the vivid color, the spontaneous, almost unfinished appearance of the weaving give it a force and directness which are lacking in many smoother and more painstaking pieces of work.

The Star of David, the Menorah, the Christian Cross, all provide the designer with ideas for beautiful hangings for temple or church.

SIGNS

Some people take astrology seriously and some only dabble at it, but almost everyone at least knows what his own sign is. The signs of the zodiac are a design challenge because it is difficult to combine in the same composition subjects as different as a bull and a virgin. Jo Dendel found that composing each sign within a circular form gave a unity to the disparate subject matter (Plate 101). In the weaving, the same colors will be used in each unit, giving further unity. The round design motifs will be in plain weave, the trapezoid background in Egyptian knot rib weave.

It was felt that the circle enclosing each motif should be really round, not wobbly. In order to weave it so, Jo drilled holes close together in the masonite loom and couched a thread around these outlines. The couching is done over the top of the warp and holds it exactly in place (Drawing 102). While couching is an embroidery device, it lends itself in weaving to making the warp more manageable. The finished units (see Plate 101) will hang in two vertical groups, six signs in each group.

CHILDREN'S DRAWINGS

Children make delightful drawings which all too often are tossed in the wastebasket because mothers do not always appreciate the direct, spontaneous quality of what children do. To transpose a child's drawing into some more permanent medium is a way to dignify what he has done. Celia Wagner's tapestry copies a drawing by a child without tampering with it in any way. We see a horse with legs like wet noodles and a tail that has slipped from

78

108. Experienced weavers like Helen Hennessey may start working on a loom without any design in mind, improvising as they go, weaving a small unit first and building on it. She calls this tapestry "Off and Away", which describes her blithe approach. Plate 120 shows fringe detail.

109. Inspired by her materials, Sharon Berg lets a few weft threads hang loose at sides of "Navajo Textures" wall hanging, to show the yarn in its natural state. Pieces of driftwood are used for accent. Plate 78 shows in detail how the points at bottom of tapestry are woven.

where tails ought to be. This is precisely part of the charm of the design and any "improving" by an adult would be sure to ruin it (Plate 103).

The technique of using a white halo effect beyond the black outline of the drawing was suggested by studying a Polish tapestry owned by the University of Wisconsin (Plate 104).

WEAVING TO DISPLAY
TWIGS AND THINGS

Weavers, so responsive to the earth's friendship offerings, can't bear to waste even a twig. And they find in weaving a way to enmesh the special twigs or sticks that come their way, too interesting to throw away. In Helen Dickey's

111. Beginning somewhere in the middle of her loom with a meandering needle, Celia Wagner evolved a boldly creative design in texture and oblique line to make this heavily fringed purse.

110. Fine red threads remain hidden in "Puff of Blue" knotted in Annabelle Bergstrom's hanging, until the close observer yields to his impulse to touch it. The surprise is quite in character with the spontaneity shown in the weaving.

weaving, the thread is almost secondary in interest to the sticks she wants to display (Plate 105). Roméo Reyna's hanging began with twigs he pruned from a bush (Plate 113).

TORN PAPER DESIGNS

One of the most effective ways to design for weaving is to tear newspaper quickly into

80

shapes. Look at each shape as you tear it. Do you tend to tear little shapes all the same size? Work at varying the sizes. Are they all similar in shape? Try notching into the edges with more careful tearing. Pierce some of the shapes by tearing holes in the interior areas. These shapes need not look like anything in nature, but some of them accidentally will. You may have started without any idea of what you wanted to do, but the shapes you tear or the shapes the torn paper makes as you assemble them may suggest your subject.

The light shapes you see in Plate 107 were torn first. No definite subject matter was in mind; in fact, several persons made a game of tearing up paper. When the papers were arranged to form some continuity over the entire area, they suggested the land patterns one sees when flying over the Rocky Mountains in a jet after some of the snow has melted, leaving the dark rocks and earth exposed on the tops of the ridges. Dark areas were then torn to support the idea. The torn paper was pinned to the warp to be used as a guide in the weaving. In the photo, the dark shapes have already been outlined with meandering (eccentric) weft and the paper removed. The colors in this particular tapestry are the blues of great expanses of clear, clean air, the whites of snow and fog and mist, the yellow greens of lichen, the forest greens of conifers, the blacks and browns of rock and earth, the purples of distant haze. The tapestry is large (4x6 feet) and is being woven by Mr. and Mrs. Roger Dunn for a particular blank space between clerestory windows in their living room. Because of the large size, the tapestry is warped on a frame of hardwood rather than on masonite. The frame will be removed when the weaving is finished.

Mike Hudson started with a lion in mind, tearing up colored construction paper to design his lion pillow (Plate 2).

112. Improvising a piece at a time on irregularly shaped looms, Winifred Roth decides later what they'll be. Her tapestry sculpture, the pieces sewed together over a wire form, combines soft blues and neutrals with black horsehair.

IMPROVISATION

Weavers who have done several tapestries, and once in a while a real beginner, can start on a loom without any preconceived idea, weave a small unit and build upon that. Helen Hennessey works almost entirely in this way. Each area she weaves makes a happening that seems to call for other happenings around it. To improvise without even a beginning sketch is perhaps the most free and creative of all ways to work. It takes a certain boldness of mind, an

innovative attitude and a willingness to fail if need be. It is like starting a journey without having any idea of destination and this requires a daring spirit and courage. Of course, if what one does is not working, one can always take it out. What that requires is the dedication of a true craftsman.

"Off and Away" by Helen Hennessey is a tapestry done in coarse white textured yarns, dark blues and purples in several weights and many tones of aqua in the background area. Plain and rib weaves mix at will and the weft is seldom at right angles to the warp except in the beginning and ending of the work. It seems to me an almost perfect example of what a good tapestry should be (Plate 108, Color 12).

Another tapestry by Helen Hennessey combines many tones of white and near-white yarns woven into brown warps that protrude in a decorative way through two bent tree branches (Plate 106). The first rows of the weaving at either end of the tapestry follow the curves of the sticks; these curves were drawn on the cardboard loom as a guide. Wrapped warps form negative shapes through which the color of the wall behind the tapestry will show.

Another weaving which "just grew" is the purse by Celia Wagner (Plate 111). It is difficult to start any motion, difficult to get any forms to "start growing" unless one *begins weaving in the central area of the warp.* The very first line of weaving may be pushed about this way and that, to establish the boundary of a form for beginning oblique movements of the weaving thread (eccentric weft).

Annabelle Bergstrom's hanging, "Puff of Blue", started with a puff of dark blue tufted knots in a field of light, heavily textured yarns

113. *Between twigs (prunings from a bush on his property), Roméo Reyna stretches a sampler's variety of weaving techniques.*

82

(Plate 110). You want to touch the woolen sheen of the knotted area and when you do, you are rewarded by the sight of fine red threads hidden among the roots of the knots. The weaver is saying in a subtle way, "Please *do* touch." The reward is more than the feel of the yarn under the fingers; there is the bonus and the surprise of the fine rich red threads which no one sees except he who looks deeply.

Winifred Roth is another weaver who starts without any notion of the finished product. Often she cuts irregular looms and after the weavings are finished and off the loom, she decides how to combine them. Sometimes she sews them together over a frame of bent wire soldered into sculptural form. Subtle variations of neutral colors and a soft blue are combined with black horsehair and coarse Mexican yarns in her tapestry sculpture (Plate 112). It has the force and mystery of the costumes and masks worn in Africa by tribal shamans.

Sharon Berg starts her weavings by contemplating the textures of coarse Navajo yarns, some of them so slightly spun they are almost fleece. By allowing the ends of some of the weft threads to hang down in a sort of bouquet at the sides of the weaving, she permits the full beauty of the yarn in its natural state to be enjoyed. Sometimes she breaks up a large area by adding warps and weaving strips that lie on top of the background color. None of these devices is planned before she begins weaving (Plate 109).

This extraneous approach turns up many surprises. It guarantees that every tapestry is one-of-a-kind. The weaver could not, and would not, copy even her own work. It is a contemporary way to work, in sharp contrast to the old custom of artist-drawn cartoons faithfully copied by artisans who patiently matched the colors of their yarns to the artists' paints.

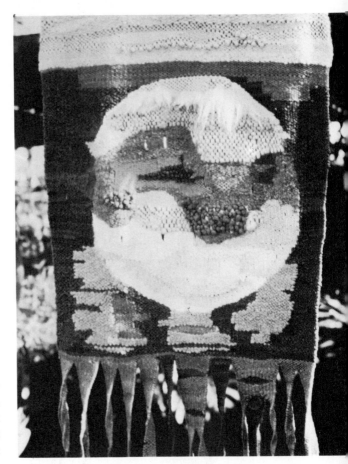

114. This 4x6' wall hanging by Roméo Reyna incorporates a mandala done in tones of blues, browns, and whites (including tufts of fur).

DESIGN IN EVERYDAY LIFE

If you were to visit the home of Roméo Reyna in Laguna Beach, California, you would find great masses of flowers blooming in unglazed stoneware pots made by the artist. The blaze of color that meets your eye comes from hundreds of fuschias, gardenias, begonias and succulents. You would be wrapped in sound from the aviary, where more than seventy finches and canaries and other exotic birds sing and nest and preen their brilliant plumage.

*115. "Setting Sun" by Roméo Reyna is a 5x7'
wall hanging with a bright red mandala woven
into a dark background. Generous use of the
tapestry slit gives the sun a shimmery texture.*

Inside the Spanish-type house, you would
find a 17th Century altar and shelves filled with
pre-Columbian art. The kitchen is a place to
linger and look and smell. A delicate aroma
comes from a wreath of braided herbs even
when nothing is cooking on the stove set above
bright Mexican tile. Everywhere throughout
the house you will find balls of bright yarn. It
is arranged in baskets, even hung from the ceil-
ing in wire containers. But to see Roméo's
weavings in process you will need to go out to
the patio because many of the works are too
large to be woven indoors. (Color Plate 10.)

One weaving was done by trimming and warp-

ing the branches of a dried Christmas tree.
Another weaving was done directly into a
wooden hoop three feet across, with fringe 60
inches long. Roméo likes the yarn spun by our
American Indians, and mohair, cow hair, rope
and silk. All his weaving is done with a needle
and most of it is in plain weave. The effects
come, not from fancy knots but from the textures of the yarns and the juxtaposition of
glowing colors. And almost always, his motif is
a mandala (Plates 114 and 115). These weavings find their way into homes and offices, into
art shows and museums across the nation and
abroad.

Roméo has trained at three art schools, but
his inspiration comes from the simple land of
his childhood. As a small boy, he swam in the
Rio Grande and brought clay from the river
bank to his Mexican grandmother who showed
him how to form it into animal shapes which
they fired in the ashes under the huge outdoor
laundry kettle. These were the beginnings of
a sophisticated artist who has successfully
bridged two cultures, two worlds and is at home
in both.

It is largely due to the encouragement and
Roméo's generous sharing of ideas that our own
craft group became so totally engrossed in
needlewoven tapestry. For many of us, tapestry
making has become almost a way of life.

We have digressed for a few paragraphs to
say something about Roméo's life-style because
we believe that the environment of an artist,
the way he sets the table and cooks his food,
the objects with which he surrounds himself
are all in some subtle way involved with what
he has to say in his work. They are just *there*
without anyone knowing how they got there.
The clay of the Rio Grande, the strings of Ruby
red peppers hung against the walls of adobe
houses, the colorful patterns of the markets of
Mexico, the potato sacks of the harvest fields
—all these have been distilled, and it is the es-
sence of these things and many more that make
the beauty and the poetry of Roméo's weaving.

10

Finishing and Hanging the Weaving

When you finish your sampler or other tapestry and it's ready to hang, lift the loops of warp out of the slits on your loom with a crochet hook. Poke any ends of yarn to the back side and weave them into the body of the weaving before snipping them off.

Some tapestries look better with a concealed hanger. When it was decided that a fringe or wrapped sets of warp would detract from Christine Cooke's tree tapestry (Plate 116), she stitched a flat, thin stick to the back (Plate 117). The stick stretches and holds the weaving to its full width as well as providing a way to hang the work. Your sampler could be hung this way.

Tess Goldsmith's tapestry is more informal in design and a purplish twig pushed through the loops of warp at the top seemed just the right hanger (Plate 119, Color Plate 6). This tapestry is weighted at the bottom with bones from a turkey neck which were bleached and then dyed with red onion skins. A few smaller neck bones are strung like beads and incorporated into the body of the weaving.

An informal bent branch seemed to fit with Jean Robinson's little weaving of a tide pool (Plate 118). Wrapped warp added at the top of the weaving gives it a larger dimension.

Wrapped warp leads to stoneware beads which weight the bottom.

Along the bottom edge of her weaving, Helen Hennessey uses a row of blue beads made of Egyptian paste, wrapping the warp below the beads instead of above them. The warp is blue and the wrapping yellow green (Plate 120).

The top of this same weaving is a polished mahogany bar drilled with holes. Each group of warps is pulled up against the bottom of the bar of wood with a cord from top (Plate 121).

To make fringe to extend the size of her tapestry, Louella Ballerino tied extra yarn into the warp loops. She tied the yarns in groups, regrouped them and tied again, and regrouped to the original position for a final tieing (Plate 122).

A weaver is bound to be on the lookout for odd objects to weight and enhance a tapestry. Junk shops, boat yards, hardware stores and old tool sheds yield unexpected treasures. Marian Sanders found just the right objects (none of us knows *what* they are) to finish off her brown and black and white, very textured hanging (Plates 123 and 124).

All but one of the weavings by our own group in this book have the warp running vertically, up and down. If the warp as it hangs seems too

*116. Tree tapestry by Christine Cook is stretched
to its full width on a concealed wood hanger.*

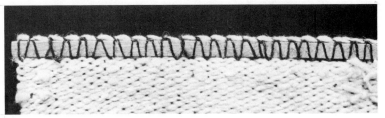

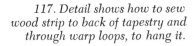

117. Detail shows how to sew wood strip to back of tapestry and through warp loops, to hang it.

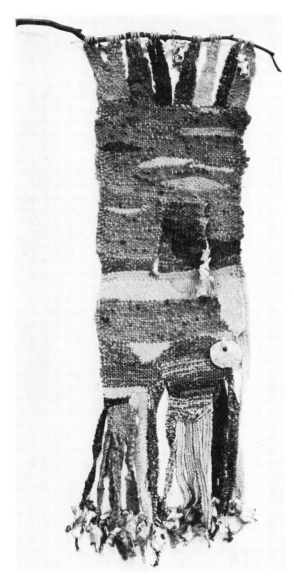

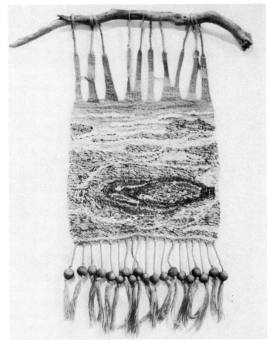

118. Wrapped warp extends the size of Jean Robinson's little tapestry, "Tide Pool". At top, it loops over driftwood hanger; at bottom, it drops to stoneware beads used as weights.

119. A twig, pushed through warp loops at top of Tess Goldsmith's "Jubilee", makes an appropriate hanger. The weights at the bottom are bleached, dyed turkey neck bones (see Color Plate 6). Collection of Mr. and Mrs. Stephen Nemetz.

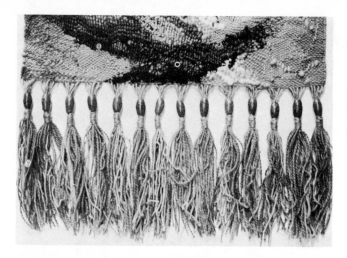

120. *Blue warp is threaded through blue beads in Helen Hennessey's "Off and Away" tapestry. Warp is wrapped below the beads with yellow-green thread, securing extra yarns for fringe.*

121. *Mahogany hanging bar at top of Helen Hennessey's tapestry is drilled with holes; a cord runs along the top threading through warp loops, pulling warp tight against bar.*

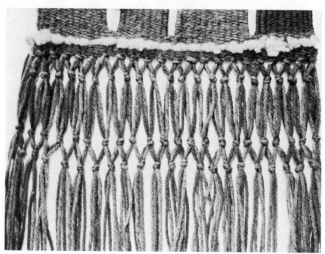

122. *Extra yarn is knotted into warp loops in Louella Ballerino's hanging and tied to make a patterned fringe.*

thin, the weaver adds to it by tying in more yarn. The exception to vertical warping among our tapestries is the child's drawing of a horse by Celia Wagner (Plate 103). The weaving from Harrania by the Egyptian children (Plate 70) also has the warp running horizontally. This is true of many tapestries done in Europe and is probably why we seldom see fringe on the bottom of contemporary European tapestry.

Whether or not one wants fringe is a purely personal decision and each tapestry is a separate problem to solve.

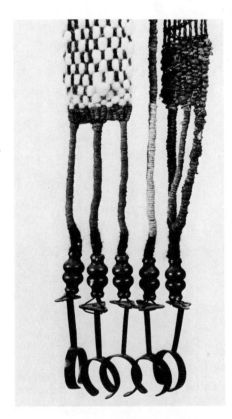

123. Detail of found objects Marian Sanders discovered and used to finish her tapestry.

124. Unusual objects weight the ends of long wrapped warp in Marian Sanders' brown and black with white tapestry. Note the variety in textures of yarn and weaves.

125. The banjo bag, designed by Lois Renwick, is woven in one piece.
It uses a great variety of materials in the off-white-beige-brown range.

11
Special Project: Banjo Bag

Using eccentric warping, Lois Renwick designed and wove a banjo-shaped bag or tote which we think has all the ideal features. The handle won't pull out or twist out of place because it is woven in. The bag is roomy, the material durable. It's easy to weave and handsome.

Make the loom for this bag out of hardboard 40 inches long; the circular part is 13 inches in diameter. Reinforce the handle area with a strip of wood on the back (Plate 126). First warping runs the full length of the loom to make the handle. It is woven before the round areas are warped. The Egyptian knot makes a sturdy weave for the handle (Plate 127).

With the handle finished, begin the eccentric warping across the body of the purse at each end of the loom. Lois used a hard linen for the warp. As soon as she laid down one area of eccentric warping, she buttonholed it tightly in the center (Plate 128). She added another area

of warping at right angles to the first and buttonholed it tightly. This buttonholing permits a view of the woven handle beneath, giving dimension to the work.

Next, Lois slipped a round ring under the buttonholed area and laid in additional warp from the edge of the purse around the ring and back to the edge. Using the ring lessens the amount of warp that would otherwise cross the center area (Plate 129).

Jute, cowhair, goathair, linen and rug yarn were woven into the warp, using both plain weave and Egyptian knot to give additional texture (Plate 130).

To complete the bag, Lois wove a boxing strip separately, sewing it between the two halves when the bag was removed from the loom. She used heavy canvas to line it. A zipper closing might be used—sew it into the lining along the straight top edge (Plate 125).

126. *Masonite loom for banjo bag is 40"*
long; handle area is reinforced with wood strip.

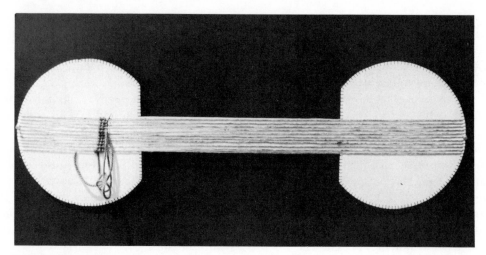

127. *Handle area is warped first and*
woven with Egyptian knot, for strength.

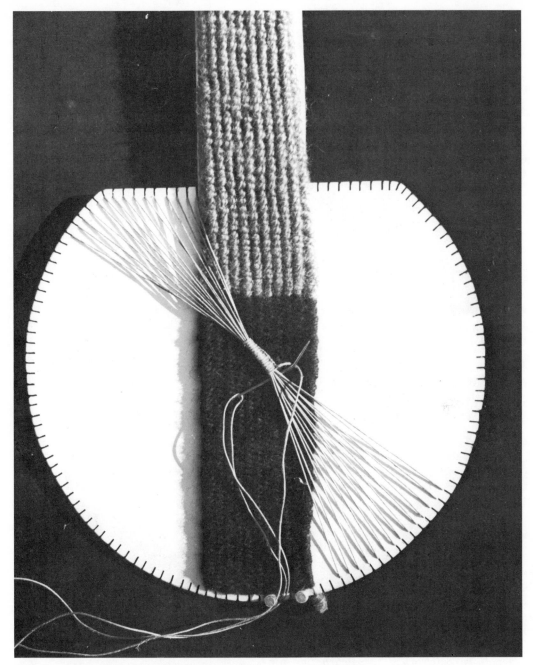

128. Eccentric warp (about 14 strands) for body
of bag is buttonholed in the center. A second
warping will be done at right angles to the first.

129. Round ring under buttonholed area holds remaining warp for the bag and permits a view of woven handle below.

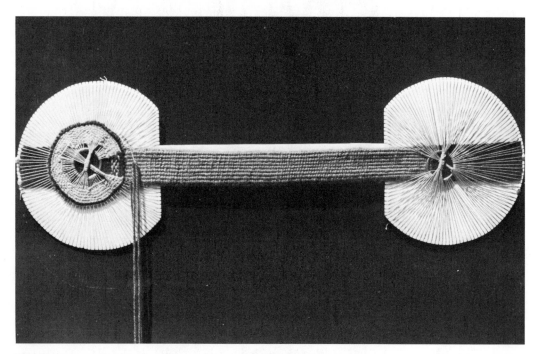

130. Bag is woven around and around on circular loom, using a great variety of materials. To complete bag, a separate boxing strip is woven and sewed to circular shapes when they are removed from the loom.